FRIENDSHIP SALAD

written by Lynn Trepicchio
illustrated by Amy Ning

HARCOURT BRACE & COMPANY

Orlando   Atlanta   Austin   Boston   San Francisco   Chicago   Dallas   New York
Toronto   London

I have the bowl.
Let's put the fruit in it.

I have the spoon.
Let's mix it all together.

Our friendship salad is done.
Let's eat!